A Cheap & C

George Wall

First off, I don't like the term 'Wild Camping'. It's camping. It's camping as it's meant to be. That thing people do at a noisy campsite, alongside a hundred other people, with a toilet block and a bingo hall, that's 'Tame Camping'. Don't even get me started on 'Glamping'.

So, from now on, let's just call it camping.

Why camp?

Well, if you're reading this, you've probably already got your own reason. And there are loads of good reasons why you should get into camping off the beaten track. For me, camping was just the next-level way for me to satiate my nature obsession. It has given me so many memorable and meaningful experiences: hearing the dawn chorus at first light on a spring morning; listening to badgers snuffle about among the bluebells on a moonless night; watching the sunset throw eerie shadows over distant tors; or staring up at the stars as they wheel across a crystal-clear sky.

But there's even more to it than that. The feeling of freedom and empowerment that you get - especially on a solo outing - can't be matched. No deadlines, no agenda, no face to be kept - just you, taking control of your surroundings, making it work.

It's the closest thing to a spiritual experience I've ever had.

Why is this the best book on the subject?

I'm a self-taught camper and I think I've learnt a thing or two. I've made a whole bunch of mistakes – some quite scary – so that you won't have to.

There are a ton of other books, YouTube videos and blogs (some of them incredibly dull) which deal with this subject, and I've ploughed through most of them so you don't have to. This is my distillation of all that knowledge.

This guide is not going to patronise you. And it's not going to bore you to death with health and safety information either. I'm going to assume that you aren't going to be daft enough to set your tent, the forest, or yourself on fire. You should probably tell someone where you're going, just in case, but if you don't want to, then - hell - that's up to you.

I'm not going to tell you to buy loads of expensive equipment. If you love your camping gadgets (and – wow – do some people love their gadgets), then good for you – go for it! But you don't need much to enjoy your camping experience.

Everything in this guide is relevant for a first time camper. It isn't going to tell you how to whittle an emergency whistle, navigate by the stars, drink your own piss, or skin a moose. It's just going to tell you what you need to get out there, and how to enjoy it.

Finally, I'm going to keep it brief. This guide is going to tell you the minimum you need to know to have a great time, then tell you to get out there and make your own mistakes.

On that note – let's go!

Preparation

Preparation for a camping expedition can be pretty fun in itself. Savour the anticipation! In the week building up to a weekend camp, I'll often find myself running different routes, meal ideas and projects through my mind.

Ideally, you should head for somewhere you've already scouted-out, but if not, you should at least look at a map or research it online.

Where to go?

The two most obvious (and excellent) places to go are Dartmoor and the Scottish Highlands; wild camping is totally legal here as long as you stay away from the roads and don't make a mess.

And you might be surprised to find that there are quite a few other places in the UK that permit wild camping. Have a look on the internet and see what's nearby: nearlywildcamping.org is a good place to start. Some places might want you to call up beforehand and ask permission, and, in my experience, they're always obliging and often quite lovely to boot.

But what if there's nowhere nearby?

The way I look at it, is that you can camp anywhere where no one is going to mind... or, better still, no one's going to know. Realistically, what are the chances of encountering someone wandering around in the middle of nowhere in the middle of the night? And then what are the chances of them having the nerve to come and tell you to move? Pretty slim.

As a general rule, I like to get away from the roads, away from the towns, and away from any private land with a big barbed-wire fence around it.

Woodland is good, as it offers a bit more privacy than, say, the middle of a field. And where there's trees, there's plenty of firewood and interesting nature to see as well.

Rivers and streams are good, too. You'll have to carry a lot to drink if you're going somewhere with no flowing water.

That said, there is a whole range of different environments to explore out there. Why not camp on the coast, or out on some open moorland? Don't be afraid to push yourself towards some new experiences.

When to go?

To start with, I'd recommend a nice warm day, after a nice dry spell in the summer. Sounds obvious, right?

But once you've got the knack, and probably got the bug, then I highly recommend trying out each and every month of the year. Each one brings its own challenges, but also a completely different set of experiences - the same patch of forest can feel like five or six completely different places over the course of the year as the patterns of light, the vegetation and the bird song all change.

What to take?

There is a bit of a trade-off here between weight and comfort: the more stuff you take, the harder the slog, but the easier your life is once you set up camp. Personally, I'm a greedy pig food-wise, and I like to take quite a few luxuries (like a good novel and some binoculars), so have trouble getting my bag down below 15kg. If you have money to spend, then you can probably shave this figure down with some super-light equipment. As a basic rule, if I can lift my pack with one arm, then I know I'm going to be able to carry comfortably it on my back.

I have divided equipment here into essential (actually essential – trust me), useful, and luxury. After a couple of trips, I'm sure you'll end up working out your own perfect 'bug-out' combo based on your preferences.

I have included my personal checklist later on.

Essential items:

<u>Clothes</u>
Yep, naked rambling is, apparently, a thing, but I wouldn't recommend it.

The trick here is layers. It's much better, in my experience, to have a thin shirt, a light jumper and a thin waterproof anorak than a great bulky coat. If you're stomping around the hills with a heavy pack on, then you have a tendency to stay warm, and you're much better off regulating your temperature by adding or removing thin layers as necessary. Each layer holds in a skin of air which heats up and keeps you cosy. You'd be surprised. Of course, if it's absolutely freezing, then you're going to need more, including gloves (I recommend fingerless, even though they make you look like a creep), a woolly hat, and a scarf. For a scarf, I highly recommend a shemagh or keffiyeh (google it and you'll instantly know what I mean), as it is really versatile and can be used as hood, picnic blanket, or improvised basket – genuinely one of the simplest but most useful things I take camping.

Waterproof trousers are a good addition, too. You can buy cheap ones (like the thin jacket mentioned above) which stuff into really small pockets. They are useful at just giving you that extra layer of warmth in the evenings, and allow you to kneel down without getting soggy knees. If it does rain, they are a godsend.

Boots are probably the one place where I would encourage you to splash out a bit (yeah, I know I said I wouldn't). A good solid pair of hiking-boots will last you years and keep your feet dry and toasty in even the worst of conditions. That said, rambling about in a pair of trainers is a curiously liberating experience when it's dry enough to do so.

Socks are nice. Mmmm, socks - nothing like changing into a pair of clean dry socks at the end of the day. Take some spares. I like to wear one thick pair (to keep my feet warm and cushioned from blisters), and a thin pair of football socks which I wear over the top. I can stretch these up over my trousers to keep the warm in and the ticks out... more on those little bastards later.

Oh, and wear some comfy undies. No one likes chafing. Top tip: don't bother bringing a change of clothes. There'll be no one about to smell you anyway.

Backpack

You'll need one of these to carry your stuff in. You'll probably struggle to fit everything in less than a 65 litre bag. A few side-pockets and zips are handy, but no need to go crazy. A lot of larger backpacks have a frame that keeps the bag off your back, which helps stop you getting all clammy and sweaty.

A bum-bag is a nice addition for stuff that you want to be able to reach easily while walking.

Tent

Bear in mind that a 'two-man tent' is actually far more like a 'one-and-a-bit man tent', and a 'three man tent' is more like a 'two man tent'. A 'one man tent' is basically a coffin. Always go one bigger than it says unless you are really tiny or actually like being cocooned.

Buy as light as you can and as simple as you can. Practise putting it up once at home or in the garden so you know what you're doing.

You may, one day, like to try out a bivvy bag, a tarp, or a hammock instead (a hammock, in particular, is divine comfort), but I recommend starting with a tent.

There are too many different tent designs to describe here, but, for me, they fall into two categories: ones that stand on their own once the poles are in, and ones where the pegs are actually an essential part of the structure (the stretching and pinning of the tent is what actually gives it its shape). Bear in mind that if you have bought the latter, you won't be able to practice putting it up in the living room, and it could be a problem if you are camping somewhere stony or frozen!

In either case, tents rarely need as many pegs as they say they do unless it's very windy. Save energy by only pegging in the essentials with the added bonus that you won't be tripping over any guy ropes.

On the subject of pegs, notice that you can push them into the ground by standing on them or, in extreme cases, by whacking them with a stick. Don't be the muppet who carries a heavy mallet out camping.

Sleeping bag

Completely essential - even in the summer. Shop about and see what you can get. They are rated in 'seasons' and usually say what temperatures they're suitable for, so get whatever is suitable for your intended adventures.

Counter-intuitively, it's good practice to stuff the sleeping bag into its pouch rather than roll it up neatly, as they last longer this way!

Roll mat

Don't do what I did at first and assume that this is some sissy luxury item. They are essential. Not only is 'the ground' a hard and uncomfortable place, but it's a cold one – sometimes very cold. A roll mat makes the difference between a good night's sleep, and lying there with chattering teeth and a sore hip wondering if you'll make it until morning.

Cheap roll mats are easy to find, and I've even seen them in pound shops for –wait for it – a pound. You can buy fancy inflatable ones, but they tend to be heavier. Although light, roll mats do take up quite a lot of space, so strap it to the outside of your pack if you have to and wrap it in a bin bag or some-such if it's wet.

Water

Well, obviously. And you'll need air, too.

Seriously, though, you need to drink plenty, especially if you're on a mission. I now know that the first sign of dehydration is getting stupid and confused. If I feel like I'm lost, it's usually because I've not been drinking enough – I sit down, drain my canteen, and have a look at my map, then I'm usually back on track. Not only that, but staying hydrated is just an all-round good thing for keeping your body working.

I recommend a simple, sturdy 1 litre plastic canteen – there's a cheap and readily available one made by 'Osprey' that the British army have been using since time immemorial in an 'if it ain't broke don't fix it' kind of way, and I can confirm that it's perfect.

Some people champion the 'camel pack', a water-filled bladder that fits into your pack and has a tube that pokes out the top for you to drink out of. I find that not only are these near impossible to refill without a tap, but that, no matter what you do, the water that comes out of them tastes of cancer.

1 litre should be plenty if you are moving through land with plenty of streams. The trick is to carry a few water purification tablets 'puri-tabs', that allow you to fill up your canteen from a stream without worrying about getting anything nasty. Just pop one in the flask and wait 30mins. They are pretty inexpensive and easy to find in hiking shops.

Food

Camping, especially if you're hiking any distance, is a hungry business, and I can't overstate how much you're going to want to eat. There's a small section on foraging later on, but, in reality, you're going to have to take the majority of your nourishment with you. Don't be afraid to pig-out - you'll likely still be losing weight even if you're stuffing away 3000-plus calories a day.

Obviously, everyone is going to have their own preferences here, but here's some general good advice:

- Although eating food cooked on an open fire is one of camping's greatest joys, you should take some food that can be eaten cold, as well - just in case you can't get one going.
- Lightweight, highly calorific food is your best bet if you're covering long distances or going out for several days. A generously-spread peanut butter and jam sandwich has almost 500 calories and travels pretty well - it comes close to the top of my list when deciding on what to take.
- Bear in mind that your backpack can be quite a bumpy, chaotic place, so stuff that can get squashed or otherwise explode in your pack is not advisable – I'm looking at you, bananas.
- Tins might seem appealing due to their longevity and indestructibleness, but they're bloody heavy. They are also quite uncomfortable sticking into your back and you'll have to carry the empties back unless you're a litterbug (in which case, I

forbid you to keep reading as you are no longer my friend).

On a personal note, I find my taste-buds seem to change when I'm out in the wild. I don't fancy pizza, choccy bars or crisps anymore, instead being drawn to more simple pleasures -nuts, dried fruits and apples (oh, sweet, juicy apples). But king of the camping foods is a sweet potato, wrapped in foil and cooked in a fire, eaten out of its own charred flesh with a teaspoon. You can thank me later.

Torch

And probably a spare torch, too, or at least some spare batteries. Nowadays, you can get insanely small, lightweight and bright LED torches for next to nothing. A head-torch is even better.

That spare torch might seem like an unnecessary item, but imagine that it's pitch black and your first torch suddenly fails; you could be stumbling around cold in the woods for hours trying to find your tent! You'll need a little spare even if it's just to change the batteries in the main one.

Map

Especially if you are taking an unfamiliar or complicated route. Getting lost is not only terrifying and dangerous, but - worse still - really embarrassing. A compass will help you get the most out of it.

Don't try and navigate by the sun or trust that moss always grows on the north sides of trees - it doesn't.

First-aid & hygiene pack

Nothing fancy, but I'd recommend a few plasters (including those expensive blister-cushioning gel ones if you can get them), sun cream, insect repellent, paracetamol, some hand-sanitizer, half a toothbrush and some toothpaste. Of course, you can chop and change depending on the situation. Try and find small containers if you can.

Oh, and tissues. Unless you're keen on getting intimately acquainted with some big leaves, you're going to need these to deal with the inevitable call of nature. Some people swear by wet wipes, but they don't biodegrade quickly like tissues do, so I avoid them.

Keys

So you can get back into your house at the end. You may also have a wallet and a phone.

Useful items:

Fire kit

Much more on fire making later. This guide doesn't cover the act of rubbing two sticks together until you make fire from scratch because, well, life's too short. For now, you'll need a little waterproof container with some matches in. It's generally a good idea to have a couple of different ways to get a fire going, so I usually pack a cheap lighter, too.

It's also worth having something to give the fire an early boost. I either pack a couple of firelighters, or some old bicycle inner-tube cut into thin strips - basically, anything super-flammable! It can be really useful if you can't find any natural kindling, or if you're just too tired or lazy after a long walk.

<u>Cooking equipment</u>

This is a classic example of the weight/comfort trade off- just think of all the items in your kitchen used in preparing a meal: knife, chopping board, garlic crusher, lemon squeezer, cast-iron non-stick pan, spatula, whisk... not to mention the little things you wouldn't even think about, like cling-film. Basically, if you start taking your kitchen with you, things will get very heavy, very fast.

If you are determined to fry something, then a small, lightweight, aluminium frying pan with a detachable handle isn't a bad bet.

Personally I have whittled my cooking equipment down to two items – 1.) A small, lightweight pot with a 'bucket-style' handle for boiling water, 2.) A kebab skewer. Cooking on a skewer is by far the lightest and easiest way to go, and saves on the washing up. Just make sure that it's long enough that you don't get burned, and that you stab it into a cork when travelling to avoid any nasty accidents!

Remember that once you've cooked your dinner, you're going to have to eat it, too, so don't forget some cutlery and plates – I simply take a teaspoon and use the lid of a Tupperware lunchbox to eat from.

If you aren't going to be building a fire (either because you are going where there's no fuel, or because you are worried about setting everything alight), then this is where your portable stove comes in. Luckily, the technology here has come on a lot in recent years and it is quite possible to get a cheap and effective cooking gadget.

The simplest and most effective of these gadgets are the small, metal spider-like attachments that screw straight onto gas canisters. While they might not be appropriate for cooking a hog roast, they are certainly effective in boiling up some noodles or making a quick cuppa. Some of these kits fit neatly, along with a standard '300' sized gas canister inside a pot. Ideal.

The other common sort of stove is the alcohol burning type, whereby you fill a little metal cup with meths and use it to cook on. In my experience, these are quite fiddly to get right and have the added danger of spilling burning alcohol onto your clothing – something that should never happen to anyone outside of a hen party.

Seat

It might sound like a bit of a luxury, but I find that a folding tripod stool (such as the type you see fishermen using) has made my adventures a whole lot more comfortable. Mine is lightweight, cost me less than £3, and straps to the outside of my pack. Perfect for sitting by the fire or just for when I stop for a rest en-route.

An alternative here might be a thick waterproof coat that you can hurl over a rock and sit on. I'll let the quality of your coat decide whether this is a good option for you.

Spare blanket

If you've splashed out on a suitably expensive sleeping bag, then this probably won't be necessary. But just like with clothing (lots of thin layers rather than one thick one, remember), this can be really comforting and gives you adaptability. I take a thin 'Tibetan style' wool blanket (you know, the sort you see in hippy market places) as a supplement to my aged sleeping bag and I'm always super toasty.

Brew kit & Thermos

There's nothing quite as invigorating as a nice cuppa on the trail, so I bring a little pouch complete with teabags and powdered milk, then use this to fill up my Thermos each morning. Finding a convenient sized container for powdered milk can be a real puzzle, but I have found that the torpedo shaped tubes you get cigars in are perfect. Coffee or hot chocolate are other pleasing indulgences. I also carry some sachets of salt, pepper and ketchup that I've nicked from pubs just in case my cooking doesn't come out quite as planned.

Penknife

This one almost made it onto the 'essential' list. A simple penknife has proved its worth a thousand times over, whether it's sharpening a stick to replace a lost tent-peg, cutting my food up, removing a splinter, or just picking my teeth.

In all honesty, unless you're going to go in for some serious bushcraft projects, you won't need anything heftier or sharper than a simple pocket knife – over the years I've bought a hunting knife, a folding-saw, and an axe - I've hardly used any of them.

Paracord

Or some other lightweight rope. Paracord is just one of those things that comes in handy. One of my most frequent uses has been to put up an improvised washing-line to dry damp items of clothing!

Luxury items:

What you take as luxury obviously depends on your own hobbies and interests - maybe you're a keen photographer, a star-gazer, or a maestro on the ukulele. It is worth noting, though, that you probably won't have as much time for these things as you'd think! Camping can be a fairly full-time occupation in itself.

Here are my suggestions:

Binoculars

Heavy, but handy. They allow you to get a bit closer to all that lovely nature, but can also prove useful when navigating and checking-out distant landmarks.

Notepad and Pencil

You'd be surprised at all the good ideas you get when you're free and wandering, so I never go anywhere without one. Doubles up as spare kindling in an emergency!

Book

If you're camping in the winter you might find yourself getting into your sleeping-bag pretty early, as you're in the dark by 5pm. A good novel is a good friend on these long evenings.

Poison

Mine's a hip-flask of single malt scotch and a cigar. The latter is useful as it keeps the midges away - or at least that's my excuse!

Tips on packing

Put the stuff you'll need last at the bottom of the pack. This tip will save you having to turn your sleeping-bag and blanket out into the mud every time you want a drink of water.

On the flip side, items like your canteen, which you will need to access throughout your day are best stashed in a side pocket where you can reach them easily. And items you might need at a moments notice, like your waterproof should be similarly stowed where they can be quickly grabbed.

If your bag's not waterproof then a couple of bin bags can be employed to store those things you *really* want to stay dry, like your sleeping-bag, fire kit and spare socks. You can buy proper 'dry bags', too, but I don't really see the point unless you actually intend to fall in a river.

Find things that fit inside other things in a 'Russian doll' kind of way to save space. For example my canteen slots nicely into my cooking pot, and my kebab skewer slides nicely into the middle of my roll mat. Also consider whether any sharp corners of lunch boxes etc. will be poking into your back!

The aforementioned bum-bag is really handy as it lets you keep your smallest and most regularly used items close to hand. If you don't like the idea of swanning around in an unfashionable bum-bag, then consider clipping it around your rucksack, essentially just creating an extra easy-to-access compartment on your main bag. Also, once you've set up camp, you can just use your bum-bag to go exploring with, thereby avoiding lugging your rucksack around any more than necessary.

A helpful system to employ is the idea of having a 'pocket carry', 'bum-bag carry' and 'pack carry'…

The 'pocket carry' is the stuff you'll keep on you at all times and want to be able to reach, perhaps your phone, keys, penknife etc.

The 'bum-bag carry' is the stuff you don't want to be rummaging around for, and probably includes the 'survival' stuff like your fire kit, some snacks, puritabs, map and compass etc.

Then the 'pack carry' covers the big stuff that you'll likely only pack and unpack once: your tent, sleeping bag etc.

Setting up camp

First off, the 'perfect spot' just doesn't exist. There is always a trade-off between several factors, and you will need to use your common sense and your judgement to find the best possible site for your tent. When you reach the general area you intend to camp in, take off your heavy bag - remember where you left it - and go for a gentle wander around the area to stake out your options. Don't rush into a decision and always be on the lookout for somewhere better. Here are the factors to consider:

The Ground

Needs to be *completely* level. Sleeping bags and roll mats are surprisingly slippery and even the gentlest of slopes will find you sliding down hill in the night, then waking up squashed in a corner of your tent. Also avoid spiky plants, jagged rocks, and puddles. Already your choices are limited!

Proximity to Water

Being near a stream or river means you won't have to go far to collect water, and can even have a paddle or a wash if it's not too cold. On the downside, however, the sound of running water can begin to play tricks on you in the night and you may end up having creepy auditory hallucinations! Also, midges and other insects like to gather around water at certain times of year. I like to camp at a point where the river is just out of earshot.

Proximity to Wood

If you have no intention of building a fire, then this isn't a consideration. But if you can pitch up where there is an abundance of dry fallen or dead-standing wood it saves you a lot of effort.

Stealth!

Even if I'm camping in a permitted area, I still like to maintain an element of secrecy. I figure that if you stay undetected then it's just polite - you aren't freaking anyone out, or ruining their nature ramble with your hobo-like appearance. Try and get a little way off the beaten track and shielded from view by trees and valleys. If you build a fire, there will be smoke, too, so maybe consider where this can be seen from.

Wind and Cold

Probably not a big issue if you are starting out with summer camping, but it's worth noting the wind direction and seeing if you can camp somewhere that is naturally sheltered. Camping on top of an exposed hill is obviously going to be a mistake, but, less obviously, camping right at the bottom of a valley can also be a problem – remember hot air rises, and the cold air scoots in underneath, so you will find that your sheltered little valley may fill with cool damp air overnight.

Dangers and Discomforts

The number one danger is falling branches – just look up before pitching tent and check if there are any ominous looking dead trees. Besides that, you don't want to set up camp anywhere that's going to flood or be involved in a landslide. Other than this, the only conceivable dangers I can think of would be posh gits with shotguns, clumsy quad-bikers or serial killers – if your camp is stealthy enough, then you've already avoided these. In terms of discomforts, mosquitoes come pretty high on the list, so note if an area seems to have a high concentration of them.

'Gut Feeling'

Don't underestimate this! Some places just feel right, and the chances are that the reason they feel right is because they are flat, well-hidden, well-sheltered, with good access to water and wood, and not swarming with midges. Let your inner caveman make a decision and the chances are you're in the right place.

Fire

No doubt about it – making a fire in the wild is one of the most satisfying things you can do. And it's eminently useful, too - it keeps you warm, cooks your food, illuminates your camp at night, keeps bugs away, and looks atmospheric. It's not as hard as you might think to build an effective and controlled fire for your purposes, but there is a knack to it, especially in damp conditions.

The General Theory

The basic principle is that you will need fuel, heat and air to build a fire. Fuel - dry, dead wood of various sizes. Heat – a match or a lighter to get it started. Air – needs to flow through your fire, so if you make it too densely packed, it just won't work.

There are loads of ways to build a fire, but I am going to describe what I find to be a simple, efficient and reliable method below. Over time, you will probably tweak this to suit your own preferences and surroundings.

George's Reliable Fire

Find a clear patch of ground which doesn't have overhanging vegetation. Ideally, scrape away any leaves so you have a patch of bare earth about the size of a small pony/large dog. Basically, make precautions not to set the forest on fire! Being near to some water is probably best if you are nervous about this eventuality.

Get an idea of the wind direction. If you can't feel it, then try dropping a little leaf or a feather and seeing where it floats. You will want to be sat facing the fire with your back to the wind so that the smoke is blown away from you. It is also worth considering where the fire is in relation to your tent, as you don't want hot embers to be blown onto it!

Gather wood. The key here, and I cannot stress this enough, is that the wood must be *dead* and *dry*. For now I'm going to assume you're making your first fire in warm, dry conditions, and I'll go into more detail on what to do if it's wet later. A good test of whether wood is dry and dead enough to burn is if it makes a loud, clean *'snap'* when broken.

The trick to efficiently gathering wood is to look for the mother lode. You can save a lot of effort (and back ache) by finding a single fallen tree instead of scraping around on the floor and collecting twigs. Use your shemagh as a sling to carry bundles of wood from point to point. Here is what you will need:

- Tinder – something super flammable to kick-start the fire. Firelighters are an obvious choice, but strips of rubber, or cotton wool covered in Vaseline are also good. If you want to use natural materials, then great! There's a little more on this later.

- **2 large handfuls** of very fine twigs – about the thickness of pencil leads. Birch twigs are fine purplish little lovelies that work perfectly for this. These will be your kindling.

- **2 large armfuls** of small twigs – about the thickness of your fingers.

- **2 large armfuls** of bigger sticks – the thickness of your wrist and above.

- Some big chunky logs (thigh thick) if you want your fire to smoulder away well into the night.

If you have found a single fallen tree, you may be able to get all of this from one place by snapping off larger branches then 'processing them down' by snapping the twigs off the branches, then the twiglets off the twigs.

Veteran twig gatherers will have learnt that there is a 'right way' to snap branches; if you have a 'Y' shaped junction on a branch, the easy way to snap is by pulling the top of the 'Y' apart, like snapping a wishbone.

Being confident and slightly violent is your best approach to gathering wood; do whatever you need from tearing off handfuls of smaller twigs, to kung-fu kicking branches, to resting larger logs over a rock and jumping on them.

Once you have your bundles of neatly graded twigs, you are ready to construct the fire itself.

Start by building a platform of wrist-thick sticks on the bare patch of ground. It should look like a little raft and be the size you want your fire to be. This is useful as you are actually starting out on a flammable surface which will burn down to ash and make a strong 'heart' to your fire. Also, the gaps between the sticks of your 'raft' allow a little air to flow underneath and help it get going.

Now get your fire lighter, rubber tube or natural tinder, light it, and put it in the middle of your 'raft'. Stay calm and don't rush.

Pick up your two bundles of very fine twigs (kindling), one in each hand, and gently place them across each other on top of your burning tinder. Again, stay cool and patient.

Very soon, the kindling will start to burn, and a nice yellow flame will poke through the top of the little 'nest' you have made.

When this happens take two big handfuls of your finger-sized twigs, and place them gently across each other on top. Make sure that you aren't bundling everything too tight and that air can flow through.

Again, the flame will grow and poke through the top of this big bundle. Add more finger thickness twigs – don't be shy - until you have a good hot fire.

Once it's roaring away and it looks like it won't go out whatever you do, then put on a bundle of the thicker sticks, or arrange them 'tepee style' around the fire. Once these are going, it's plain sailing and the fire will burn as long as you keep feeding it.

Wet Weather

Wet weather fire making is really tricky and requires a lot more time and effort, especially in the preparation stages.

The principle is the same, but you need to be very selective in the sticks you gather. The trick is to ignore anything on the floor and, instead, search the branches of other trees for dead wood that has fallen and become suspended there (top tip - those little birch twiglets often get caught in holly bushes). Even then, not all of this will be dry, and much will need to be discarded. Look for dead trees that are still standing - 'dead-standing wood', as these can be quite dry if they've been sheltered from the rain.

Once you've gathered your bundles of wood, you need to keep them dry, so don't just plonk them down in a puddle on the floor!

If you manage to get enough dry wood to get the fire started, the trick is to build a fire that's furious enough to dry out wet wood – think big! I place larger damp sticks and logs around the fire in a 'Jenga' like formation (remember that air must be able to flow) so that they dry out before they are added to the fire.

Natural tinder and different types of wood.

As you get more acquainted with fire making, you might notice that some wood burns much better than others. This is because different trees have different burning properties - quite interesting, really!

Probably the most useful tree to know is the birch. Birch trees have silver-white, papery bark, with younger twigs being a deep purplish colour. Birches are full of natural oils which burn like crazy, and are probably your best friend when getting a fire started. If you find dead birch trees where the bark is peeling off in papery strips, you will find that this bark is an excellent fire lighter, especially if you shred it up into thin strips. The only downside to birch is that it burns really fast, so you will need to gather lots if there are no other woods to complement it.

Another good burner is pine, which not only burns hot and fast, but has lovely-smelling smoke. Insects can't abide the smell of burning pine, so this is another bonus. Dry pine-needles also make great natural tinder.

Oak, with its knobbly twigs and Mr. Jelly-shaped leaves is another useful one to know. It doesn't burn anywhere near as easily as birch or pine, but once it's going it burns hot and for a long, long time.

A Brief Health and Safety Note

I'm not worried about you hurting yourself – you're much too sensible for that. But I am a little worried you might get carried away and set the woods on fire. That would be awkward, wouldn't it?

In Britain, this is only going to be an issue in that two day period once a year when everything is actually tinder dry. If it is like this, then you will need to be sensible and pay extra attention to the wind direction, as you don't want hot embers landing in a big pile of dead leaves.

In this sort of situation, you will also need to make extra sure that your fire is out when you are done. This can require a surprising amount of water, so a nearby river or stream will be useful (though peeing on a fire to put it out is surely one of the most liberating things you can attempt).

The only other hidden fiery pitfall I can think of is peat. Large areas of Dartmoor, for example, have peaty soil, and if this is dry, the ground itself is flammable, so be extra careful if this is the case!

To minimize the ecological damage I'm causing, I always look for previously used fire pits as a first choice. If not, then the areas of bare ground you can find under beech or holly trees are good guilt-free places to build a fire.

Food

Cooking on an open fire is one of the great joys of camping, and it tastes great, too. It is hard to say how much of this is due to the 'smoked' flavour of food cooked over the fire and how much is psychological – the deep satisfaction of hot food eaten in the fresh air after a long day's trekking and fire building!

The three main ways to cook over a fire are boiling in a pot, roasting on a skewer or baking in foil, and all require a few skills:

Skewer

As mentioned earlier, this is by far the easiest way to do things. The trick is to cook over hot coals rather than open flame.

So, let your fire burn for at least an hour until it has become well established and a really hot 'heart' of glowing coals, then scrape some of it them into the open (it is nice to keep one area of your fire burning properly while you do this). Now you will have a bed of glowing hot embers which are perfect for cooking.

Lie two thick sticks either side of your coals and place the skewer over these as you would over a barbeque. Easy!

Recipe idea: try cooking chunks of halloumi, cherry tomatoes, slices of courgette, pepper and mushroom using this method, then slide them into a pitta bread. Alternatively, just whack two skewers through some sausages (like you are making a ladder with meat rungs) then eat them in a sandwich with lots of stolen ketchup sachets.

<u>Baking in foil</u>

Another straightforward method and particularly good with potatoes – have the food ready-wrapped in your pack.

Simply chuck the foil-wrapped goodies into the heart of a roaring fire and turn them over every 15 minutes or so using a couple of long sticks. Some people like to use the hot coals method for potatoes too, but I find the coals cool off long before the food is cooked.

Recipe idea: the aforementioned sweet potato! Wrap it, chuck it in, then rescue it 45 mins later. Even the burnt skin will taste amazing. If that's too exotic, then you can do something with a standard potato, but it'll take twice as long to cook. I'd also advise retrieving your potato early, cutting it open and applying butter and seasoning, then rewrapping and giving it another ten minutes in the flames.

Boiling in a pot

Unless you've invested in a portable stove, boiling water can be a surprisingly difficult task out in the wild, but is an essential skill if you want a cuppa in the morning. 'Boil in the bag' meals, or simple foods like pasta, rice, and instant noodles are good camping foods if you like to cook this way.

To boil water you will need a pot with a handle allowing you to dangle it over the fire. If the pot has a lid, this will massively speed-up the boiling time. Also, only boil as much as you need as the more water you try and heat the longer it will take.

Getting the pot suspended at the right height is the tricky part, and probably best arranged *before* you actually start the fire. You will need to find a thick Y-shaped stick and another strong straight one to use as a pole. Sharpen the bottom of the 'Y' by cutting *away* from you with your pen knife (please don't cut yourself), then stab it into the ground near your fire. Lay the pole stick through the crux of the 'Y' and hang the pot on the end. You may need to put something heavy on the ground end of the pole to stop it falling into the fire, or use some spare tent pegs to pin it down. This technique is economical and straightforward, but does require quite a lot of tweaking to get a stable arrangement the right height from the fire (i.e. not so close that you smother it and not so high that it never boils). Don't get demoralised – just fiddle about until you have a working arrangement.

If you really don't care about your cooking equipment, then you may be able to just shove the pot into the fire. This will result in it becoming completely blackened, but can be surprisingly effective.

Be prepared to wait at least 10-15mins to get your boiling water.

Recipe idea: cheap packs of instant noodles with a sachet of seasoning are lightweight and easy to cook – ideal camping food! You can even make your own chopsticks by scraping the bark off two green twigs of the correct proportions. I like to make my noodles fancier by adding some foraged goodies: stinging nettles, primrose and dandelion leaves, wood sorrel, or even some wild mushrooms!

Which leads me neatly on to…

Foraging

Foraging is a really satisfying activity when out camping, and a good way to get some extra calories, vitamins, or just flavour, without carrying extra food with you. Foraging is a huge topic and there are lots of great books on the subject. Here, I will just touch on some of the easiest, safest and commonest wild foods around.

No need to worry about poisoning yourself, just don't eat anything you aren't 100% certain of. The trick is not to pick loads of random stuff then try and identify it later (doubtless gathering lots of poisonous stuff along the way), but to go out with a few edible species in mind and gather only these.

Here are my top 'wild edibles':

<u>Stinging Nettles</u> – Can be boiled or simply wilted over the fire – their sting vanishes when heated. They taste like spinach, but nicer, and with a slightly more fluffy texture. Pick only the small leaves from the top of the plant and blow on them to dislodge any ladybirds and aphids at the gathering stage. The downside? You will need gloves.

<u>Wood Sorrel</u> – Looks like lime-green clover growing in woodland, often around the base of trees. Has a delicious, zesty kind of flavour and goes well, I find, in puddings. Simply gather it up, leaves and stem, give it a wash and nom away.

<u>Wild Garlic</u> – Large, glossy, dark green, blade-shaped leaves that grow straight out of the ground with (at the right time of year) clusters of small white flowers. Also, they smell, as you might imagine, of garlic! The best way to use these is to simply shred some leaves into a dish to give a garlicky flavour, though the flowers and roots are also edible.

As a bonus, ticks and other insects supposedly hate the smell of garlic, so crushing a bit and rubbing it on your ankles and wrists (or simply eating lots of it) may help in preventing insect bites. I'm not sure how thoroughly scientific this information is, but it seems to work for me.

<u>Blackberries</u> – Yep, you know these. Surprisingly few berries are actually edible or palatable to humans, so it's a delight to find that our most common one is delicious!

Hazelnuts – Less rare than Walnuts and less hassle than Chestnuts. Make sure you are familiar with the hazel leaf to identify – they are roughly oval, with jagged edges and a distinctive little point at the end. The nuts themselves get eaten up by squirrels pretty quickly, so don't expect to find large quantities of ripe nuts on the ground. Instead, get there earlier in the year and pick the young green nuts. Just get the shells off and scoff them!

There's a trick to getting into these – use your penknife to shave off the very bottom of the nut until you see a thin, straight crack, then poke the knife in and twist to lever the shell open.

Chanterelles – A delicious and easily identified mushroom. Chanterelles are small, uniformly orangey in colour and a 'flattened trumpet' shape. They have very shallow grooves which run from under the cap down the stem where they merge quite unlike the gills of supermarket mushrooms. They smell a little of buttery apricots!

There's something satisfying about tucking into a big dish of Chanterelles around the fire, knowing that people are paying through the nose for them in a fancy restaurant somewhere.

A very decadent wild camper might carry a little bottle of garlic infused oil with them just in case they stumble across some of these little beauties.

<u>Porcini</u> – There's little more satisfying than running across a big porcini! Porcinis have a fat 'stem' and a large reddish-brown cap. They have pores under the cap rather than gills. Most species of Porcini are edible, but for simplicity's sake, stay away from any which turn blue when cut into as these can be poisonous. Scrape out the pores before cooking and check carefully for maggots etc.

Bad things that can happen and how to avoid them

In this section I'll discuss some of the common pitfalls that can catch-out novice campers. I've learnt from my mistakes, so you don't have to!

Getting cold

If you are moving, you are unlikely to get cold, especially if you have a heavy pack on. If you do, then it's simply a case of adding layers, as even thin ones make a big difference.

You are in much more danger once you stop, and especially at night. Here are some tips to stay warm when getting to sleep:

Firstly, make sure you are sleeping off the ground by using a roll matt – this can't be emphasised enough, as you lose a massive amount of heat from contact with the cold ground.

Secondly, go to bed warm. Obviously, a fire will help, and even the process of gathering wood will help you warm up, but sometimes it's just too damp to make a fire, in which case you can have a quick jog on the spot before getting into your sleeping bag! Having a belly full of food and being well-hydrated helps, too.

Thirdly, pile on the layers. Getting into your sleeping bag with all your clothes on is not only uncomfortable, but strangely ineffectual. You are much better piling the clothes on top of the sleeping bag once you're in. I like to push the bottom end of my sleeping bag into my zipped up jacket which keeps my feet warm, then pile any other clothes (and a spare blanket) on top of myself.

Getting hot

This guide is intended to help with wild camping in the UK.

Getting lost

Even if you have a map and a compass, you can still get disorientated, especially if you are moving through thick woodland, or in an environment like Dartmoor where the pixies can alter reality and distort the shape of the land. An old folk tale says that if the pixies are leading you astray you should turn your coat inside out, but the following suggestions are even more useful:

Retrace your steps. Some of the worst instances of getting lost are due to stubborn pig-headedness and forging on when you've clearly gone wrong. Swallow your pride and retrace your steps to the last place where you were certain of your position. Yes, even if it is uphill.

Find a vantage point. I don't recommend climbing a tree, but the view from atop a hill can give you some valuable clues to your position.

Find a landmark. Maps include features like copses, rocky outcrops and rivers which will all help you find where you are. Rivers, especially, are useful as you can move downhill until you find them then follow them either up or downstream to somewhere you recognise.

Paths go somewhere. As a general rule, anyway! Learn to recognise if a path is used by people or just a deer-run by looking for footprints and cleared foliage above waist height. If you follow a path, you'll end up somewhere that humans use.

The main thing is to stay calm. Make sure you are well hydrated and thinking clearly, and you'll find your way. It's all part of the adventure!

<u>Getting bitten</u>

Midges and mosquitoes can be a massive pest on camping journeys at certain times of year. The obvious solution is to use insect repellent (the stronger the better – just don't get it in your eyes or mouth), but there are a few other helpful things you can do.

Supposedly, most insects can't abide the smell of garlic, so a strong garlicky meal before (or during) a camping trip might help.

Smoke is another fantastic insect repellent - pine smoke especially. Once you've got a fire going you will have little trouble with insects. If you smoke, then a cigarette or cigar is also effective.

Certain times of the day are more midge-infested than others, most notably the hour before dusk. A good tip is to be moving around at this time – maybe a nice evening walk – rather than sitting still and getting eaten alive!

Getting bitten by ticks

Ticks are tiny spider-like insects which live on the ground and in bushes and will climb onto you at any opportunity, where they will crawl up your arms or legs and find a nice spot to latch on and suck your blood. At certain times of year they can be quite numerous. It is important to remove the ticks with tweezers by *twisting* them so they are forced to let go, otherwise the minute jaws can be left in your skin where it can become infected. I'm itching just writing about this!

I have found that rolling my socks over my trousers and tucking in my shirt avoids the majority of ticks getting at me. The main time that I find them is when collecting wood, as I am forced to reach onto the ground and bushes to gather twigs; fortunately, ticks rarely actually bite your hands, so if you check regularly, you catch them crawling up your arms and flick them into oblivion.

Not only is being bitten by a tick disgusting and really itchy, but it can carry the (very small) danger of catching Lyme disease – no laughing matter. If you develop a weird rash after being bitten by a tick, get it checked out as soon as possible, as Lyme disease is treatable when caught early.

Another good trick is to go camping with someone tastier than yourself.

Needing a poo

Ah, the inevitable call of nature. Chances are, you are going to need to vacate your bowels at some point on a camping trip – something which causes some people all sorts of difficulty and embarrassment.

But no need to worry. If you are remote enough then no one is going to see you, and it isn't as bad as you'd think. Just make sure you aren't squatting in long grass of ferns where those ticks can get to your nether regions.

Some people might like to take a light plastic trowel to bury their leavings, but I find this isn't necessary. Poop and tissue paper (not wet-wipes) rot away in a couple of days, or even quicker if it rains. Just be conscious of others - go somewhere discreet and off the path, and, ideally scrape some leaf-litter over it.

Taking other people camping

This might seem like a really good idea. But think carefully. 'Wild' camping is actually a pretty niche activity, and just because you like it doesn't mean others will. I have pretty mixed experiences of taking others camping and have a few tips for you.

Firstly, make sure people know exactly what to expect. And 'manage expectations' – don't build up their hopes that it will be a utopian paradise! Much better that they don't expect too much, and are pleasantly surprised rather than the other way around. I suggest getting them to sign a waiver along these lines:

Wild camping is a strenuous activity and may involve any or all of the following: getting cold, getting hot, getting achy legs, carrying a heavy pack, needing a poo, getting bitten by insects, being a bit hungry, being a bit thirsty, getting a bit bored, being tired, not getting enough sleep, or getting 'freaked out' by noises in the night. I, the undersigned, promise to endure these hardships with the minimum of whingeing.

Not really. But you get the point!

Secondly, make sure your 'guests' are well equipped. Once you've practiced camping for a while, you'll probably have accumulated a few spare bits and bobs. Make sure they don't skimp on important items like water bottles and roll mats. Why not lend them this guide? Or, better still, get them to buy their own copy!

Thirdly, be prepared to alter your plans and normal routine to accommodate newbies. Have a plan which involves less walking than normal and perhaps avoids anywhere where stealth is required – some campers, for example, might like to play music on their phones when they get to camp rather than revelling in the majestic silence of nature. Basically, put others' needs before your own and you are more likely to give your pals an enjoyable experience.

My Kit List

Rucksack (Carrion 65litres):

Tent (Vango Banshee 200)

Sleeping Bag (Coleman)

Roll Mat (Cheap, foam)

Spare Blanket (Thin, woollen)

Folding stool

Waterproof cagoule, & waterproof trousers

2X Kebab skewers stabbed into a cork

2X large Tupperware boxes of food, and 1X small Tupperware container of nuts and dried fruit

Thermos flask (750ml)

Hip flask of whisky

Brew kit (teabags, powdered milk, teaspoon, other condiments etc.)

Cooking pot

Canteen (Osprey 1l)

Woolly jumper, fingerless gloves and a woolly hat
Spare socks

Shemagh

Head torch

Notebook and pencil

Binoculars

Novel

Plastic bag for rubbish

Bum-bag:

Map

Compass

Paracord

Penknife

Hygiene/Aid tin (plasters, paracetamol, puritabs, 1/2toothbrush, toothpaste, hand sanitizer, tissues)

Fire-making tin (lighter, matches, strips of inner tube)

Spare torch

Cigar

Example Camps

Here are two short stories of camping trips as examples of the sorts of experience you can have. I'll describe my worst ever and best ever camp to give you an idea of the range of experiences available.

My worst camping trip ever

This was the first 'wild camping' trip I attempted. It's a wonder I carried on at all! If only I'd had some sort of useful guide to help me out...

It was early spring and the weather was cold and damp. I decided I'd like to explore an area near Ivybridge on Dartmoor and camp overnight in an old oak woodland where I might see some owls or birds of prey.

I got a lift up there with a friend (who wouldn't be camping out) and planned to get a train back to civilisation the next day. We walked quite a way together, then he turned back mid-afternoon.

I carried on without him and hit an unexpected dead-end: a load of private land and big fences. I didn't have a map as I thought I'd remembered the route pretty well (just follow the river), and figured I could use my phone to look at Google Maps in an emergency. There was, of course, no signal.

I ended up retracing my steps, then taking a different route that got me even more lost. I only found my way back to a recognisable point by walking along a road – not very 'wild'.

It was getting late. I decided to cut my adventure short and head back to the train. This was quite a slog over the moor - further than I'd realised - and I was already tired due to my unplanned detour, and a load of unnecessary crap in my rucksack weighing me down. I couldn't check train times because there was still no signal. Eventually, exhausted, I made it to the station. It was Sunday. I'd missed the last train.

I would have to head back up onto the moors and make camp. By now it was just beginning to get dark, my feet were killing me, and I knew I had a serious hill to climb just to get to the moors, let alone a suitable camping spot.

When I eventually got to the moor, I stumbled on a great looking spot – a little close to civilisation, maybe, but pretty good. It was an old mine working that left some huge dips in the ground. I'd be well concealed and sheltered there! When I reached it and peered over the lip, it was filled with dodgy-looking youths chucking rocks at bottles. Perhaps not. I slunk off.

By now, the light was fading. I made it a little further onto the moor and set up camp by a little stream. I wasn't concealed as well as I'd have liked, and wasn't entirely sure if I was allowed to camp there, but I was knackered, so I had no choice.

I got the tent set up without too much difficulty, but making a fire was out of the question – it was too damp, there were no trees about, and I was too grumpy and tired anyway.

Sitting in the doorway of the tent, looking out at the last of the light, what looked like a huge greyhound appeared along the bank of the stream. My heart was in my mouth. I thought a farmer was about to come and move me on, or, worse, I was about to be savaged by the Hound of the Baskervilles. It trotted closer, and in the dim light, I realised it was a deer! It stopped only about 10ft from my tent to drink from the stream. It was completely oblivious to me until I shifted my weight and scared it off. This was the one good thing that happened.

Time for bed. I had no roll mat and it was getting seriously cold. The ground seemed to radiate cold straight into me and sleep was nearly impossible. When I did, intermittently, doze off I would wake shivering and numb. It was a wretched night.

The next day, there was a frost on the ground. I was so cold and miserable that I didn't bother with breakfast, seeing any nature, or enjoying the sunrise, I just trudged back into town. A farmer on a quadbike drove by and laughed at me.

My best camping trip ever

What a difference a few years' experience makes! It's hard to pinpoint which adventure has been my best, but this recent one certainly sticks out as a contender.
It was a beautiful mid-summer's day on a Friday afternoon. A few colleagues and I had been talking about going camping for ages, and finally an opportunity had arisen.

We arrived at a popular riverside spot on Dartmoor in the early evening, knowing that it wouldn't be dark until gone 10pm. As some people were sharing tents, and we'd be able to share some other equipment, we were able to take more luxury items than usual – plenty of beers, our swimming stuff, and a guitar!

I'd walked the route alone a couple of times, so knew it wasn't an overly challenging walk, and had even scouted out the best place to set up camp. It involved crossing the river at an unlikely place, so the chances of bumping into anyone was exceptionally slim.

When we got to camp we were hot from walking and carrying our packs, so immediately got into our swimming gear and jumped into the river – there was a beautiful, deep natural bathing pool with smooth rocks to sit on and even mossy slides that acted like flumes in a leisure centre. We bobbed about drinking beer and joking.

With the last of the light, we dried off, set up out tents and gathered materials for a fire. We were in a wood, and there was an abundance of fallen birch, oak, and holly all around. Between us it was light work. We cleared a big space of ground where the fire wouldn't cause any damage, and got it going.

We spent the evening around the fire eating, drinking beer, and playing the guitar. We had all brought different food and ended up sharing various courses of sweet potato, veggie sausages, kebabs and pasties.

After midnight, a little drunk, we decided to go back in the water. It was a great decision! Although it was cold, the treeless space above the river revealed a sky swimming with stars. There, floating in the blackness with the depth of the sky extending, infinite, above us, we felt a genuine connection to something primal and spiritual.

After our swim, we were able to dry off and warm up around the fire. More eating and drinking!

We started the next day with another swim, and munched on leftovers for breakfast. At our leisure, we packed up our tents and rubbish, scattered the cold ashes of the fire, covered our tracks and made our way home.

30 Camping Tips & Ideas

1.) If you are brave, consider trying a Bivvy Bag. Basically this is a very light weight waterproof sleeping bag that you can put your normal sleeping bag inside. No need for a heavy tent! You will still need your roll mat though. I only advise Bivvies in the best of weathers.

2.) If you are flamboyant, try camping with a hammock. They are very comfy compared to other sleeping systems, but require you to learn a few knots, so are less simple. You will also need to be going somewhere with trees, obviously.

3.) If you fancy going old-school, consider buying a 'shelter half'. Shelter halves are outmoded pieces of military kit (usually cold war era) which you can pick up in army surplus stores - they are essentially a big cape, something between a tent and a coat. Although heavy, a shelter half is a multi-purpose item that works as a blanket, coat, ground sheet, picnic blanket, tarp etc. Mine is a Polish type called a Lavvu and I love it.

4.) Try combining camping with mountain biking for a real adrenaline adventure. However, you will need to find a way to get some of the weight off your back by buying some bags that attach directly to your bike. Bear in mind that when 'bike packing' you will be a lot heavier than when you are just cycling normally, so don't be over-ambitious.

5.) If you need to cross a river, pack some cheap flipflops by shoving them down the side of your backpack. Crossing a river is always harder than you think, even if shallow, and not having to worry about sharp rocks is one less problem. They are also a convenient half way house back into your boots.

6.) If you're thinking of combining your wild camping with some wild swimming – great combo! Then buy a travel towel. Normal towels are too big, and the specialist, lightweight microfibre towels don't work.

7.) Learn to put up a washing line made out of paracord. You will need to learn a 'thief's knot' (sounds cool, right), and an 'adjustable hitch' (less so). This has been invaluable to me so many times, either for drying out a damp sleeping bag, for drying my tent before packing away, or just for hanging things on so I don't lose them. Always leave *something* on the line when it is up or else you risk accidentally garroting yourself by walking into it.

8.) Football socks can be pulled up over your trousers to keep ticks out. They also keep your shins warm.

9.) If it's a nice day, but it's damp after rain, consider collecting your wood early and stacking it so that it dries out in the sun or wind. Surprisingly effective!

10.) A pencil sharpener can be used to shave down little twigs and create kindling for fires. Also useful for sharpening your pencil.

11.) Use hairbands and headbands as convenient ways to keep things rolled up in your pack. Roll mats, blankets, shemaghs and coats all benefit from this treatment. You can toss all these various scrunchies into your sleeping bag pouch to keep them safe once you're unpacked.

12.) Raid old fires. Perhaps not the most 'wild' way to do things, but you will often find the remains of others' camps, and these will often have a little pile of unused or half burnt sticks. It would be a shame to let all their hard work gathering them go to waste.

13.) Master the Ivenk fire. This is the best type of fire you can make as it's hot, not smoky, and requires less maintenance than a normal teepee fire. Basically, build your normal fire, then use a really big log as a 'back wall' to reflect the heat back towards you. You can then lay other thick branches so that they poke out over the big log so their ends catch fire like big cigars pointing towards you. Getting the wind direction right is essential for this fire (it should be blowing from behind you onto those 'cigar ends' then bouncing heat back towards you off the 'back wall' log).

14.) Learn to identify trees. This is useful if you are building a fire, as some woods burn much better than others. Identifying trees by their leaves is the easiest method.

15.) If you have a regular spot, you might consider hiding some items out there to make your future journeys very light and efficient! Stash your stuff in a big green drybag and hide it well. Eventually this will start to leak, so you will need to buy another drybag and nest it inside the first… and so on.

16.) If you regularly visit the same spot for camping, consider leaving the best wood for when you really need it. It might be a pain collecting dead wood off the floor, but if it's dry enough for this, then you can save that perfect dead-standing tree for when you really need it in the long soggy British winter.

17.) Make a portable portion of toothpaste by snipping a couple of inches of plastic drinking straw, then poke it into your tube of toothpaste. You can then burn both the ends closed to seal in the single portion.

18.) I'm strongly anti wet-wipe, but you can get moist tissue that is biodegradable if that's your thing.

19.) When you unroll your roll mat, roll it completely the other way first, so that it stops coiling up.

20.) When pulling out your tent pegs, use the first peg as a hook to haul the others out of the ground.

21.) If you are boiling some water for tea or noodles, boil some extra and use it to wash your hands and face after dinner. You will instantly feel human again!

22.) If you have a spork, snap it in half to make a spoon and a fork.

23.) Little bottles for milk, sauce, or oil are very useful. The kinds you get in gift sets of whisky miniatures are ideal. Put them on your birthday list and dispose of the contents responsibly before repurposing.

24.) Learn some whittling skills. This can be helpful for making any items you have left behind, say tent-pegs or cutlery.

25.) Get a stick. Ideal for prodding soft ground, keeping your balance across logs, whacking back holly bushes and poking suspicious mushrooms. If you have developed some whittling skills, you can shave off the outer bark and make it ergonomic.

26.) Take note of sunset and sunrise times before you head off on an adventure. It's good to know when you need to be set up by, especially in the winter!

27.) Make an established peeing zone when camping as a group so that you don't end up picking sticks up out of someone's wee. Don't always wee in the same place as it can be damaging to moss and other plant life.

28.) Use your camping trip as a complete 'digital detox'. Start by turning off your phone, but consider taking this even further – I generally refuse to even take photos, instead preferring to be 'in the moment' rather than trying to get an image to look at later.

29.) Don't survive. Well, do *survive*, obviously. I just mean don't get into a situation where you need to survive. Plan for an easy life rather than attempting anything unnecessarily macho. The little 'survival kits' that you can buy are almost entirely useless.

30.) Find more detail on these tips, and more, in my 2nd book – 'A Cheap and Cheeky Guide to Wild Camping 2'!

Printed in Great Britain
by Amazon

35278095R00036